How do I feel about

LOOKING AFTER MYSELF

Sarah Levete

COPPER BEECH BOOKS • BROOKFIELD, CONNECTICUT

Designed and produced by
Aladdin Books Ltd
28 Percy Street
London W1P 0LD

First published in the United States
in 1998 by
Copper Beech Books,
an imprint of
The Millbrook Press
2 Old New Milford Road
Brookfield, Connecticut 06804

Printed in Belgium
5 4 3 2 1

Designer   Tessa Barwick
Editor   Jen Green
Illustrator   Christopher
                O'Neill
Photographer   Roger Vlitos

**Library of Congress
Cataloging-in-Publication Data**
Levete, Sarah
Looking after myself / [Sarah Levete].
p. cm. — (How do I feel about)
Includes index.
Summary: Discusses aspects of health
and safety such as keeping safe while
playing, healthy eating, and dealing with
emotional problems.
ISBN 0-7613-0809-1 (lib. bdg.)
1. Children—Life skills guides
—Juvenile literature.
[1. Health. 2. Safety.] I. Title. II. Series.
HQ781.44 1998   97-41644
613.6'083—dc21   CIP AC

Contents

Introduction

Join Marsha, Jamie, Nicky, and Ben as they talk to you about the different ways that they look after themselves. From Ben's magic recipe for a healthy body to Marsha's tips on dealing with bullies, Marsha, Jamie, Nicky, and Ben will give you hints on ways to keep happy and safe.

Take care. keep safe.

Jamie

If it feels wrong, say "NO!"

Nicky

Look after your body.

Marsha

Eat well, play safely, have fun!

Ben

Happy and Healthy

Before bed, Ben and Nicky wash up. Ben is telling Nicky that he won the relay race at school. Nicky says all that exercise has made him a bit smelly, so he can shower first.
A clean body is a happy and healthy body. Can you think of any other ways you can look after your body?

Your feet need a wash, too!

Sing while you wash!

◀ *Teeth Forever*

Teeth are fussy. They need brushing twice a day — after breakfast and before bed. For a dazzling smile, save candy and sugary drinks for special treats.

Clean Hands ▶

Germs are tiny living things that can give you coughs or stomach aches. The good news is they don't like soap and water!

Wash and dry your hands before each meal and after you go to the bathroom. This will help keep germs down the drain, where they belong!

▲ *What A Smell!*

After a day playing, a shower or bath helps to wash away dirt. It gets rid of nasty odors, to make sure you smell nice!

Remember your hair, too. It needs a brush twice a day.

If your head feels itchy, tell your mom or dad who will help you to get rid of any itchiness.

1. Paul spent all his allowance on candy. He did not want to share it.

2. Paul ate the whole bag of candy. He dropped the wrappers on the ground.

3. Paul's teeth keep the dentist very busy!

Why did Paul have to see the dentist?

He ate too much candy. Candy tastes nice but it is not very kind to teeth. Try and eat candy for treats only — it will taste even better! Always remember to put your litter in the trash can.

For a healthy body, from the top of your head to the tips of your toes, eat potatoes, rice, bread, or pasta with meat, fish, cheese, or beans. And lots of fruit and vegetables. Delicious!

▽ Sweet Dreams

Your body works day and night to keep you healthy. After a busy day, it needs peace and quiet to give you energy for tomorrow.

So, shut your eyes and dream… Goal!

◁ Fun And Fit!

Did you know that it is good for you to play in the park? Exercise keeps you fit, so get moving! But always remember to tell an adult where you are.

Here is Ben's magic recipe for a happy and healthy body!

"At meal times, eat the foods that give you lots of energy. But remember to wash and dry your hands before going to bed!"

Can you think of any other ways to keep happy and healthy? What about a good night's sleep?

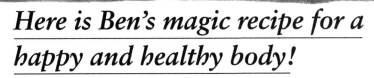

7

Having Fun

Last week, Jamie was showing off. He climbed to the top of a tree. But he fell off and cut his knee — it really hurt. Marsha was not impressed. She knows that play is only fun if it is safe. How do you have fun and keep safe?

Tips For Fun Without Tears!

Always remember to cross a street at a crosswalk, even when you're rushing for an ice cream!

Keep away from railroad tracks or building sites — they can be very dangerous. When it's dark, play inside — it's safer, and you can see what you're doing!

Put away toys so you won't trip over them.

Marsha, what do you think about safety rules?

"All the do's and don'ts can get boring. But remember that they keep you safe so you can have fun.

A rule is easier to follow if it makes sense. So, if you don't understand a rule, ask."

9

Out and About

Nicky and Jamie are going to buy a birthday present for Ben. Nicky says they need to make sure they have enough money for the phone, just in case of an emergency. Do you know how to stay safe when you are out and about? Find out on the next pages.

1. Jo was out with her dad and sister.

2. Jo couldn't find her dad in the store.

3. A kind-looking lady offered to help. Jo did not know her.

What do you do if you get lost?

Don't panic! Even though it can be scary, there are several things you can do.

Stay where you are, so that your mom or dad can come back and find you.

If you can't see a police officer, go into a store and ask the assistant to help.

If a stranger offers to help, ask him or her to find a police officer. But don't go off with the stranger by yourself.

"You haven't got enough for all of those."

"Let me buy them for you. It's OK. I know your mom."

1. Tim was in the store, buying candy with his allowance.

2. A man offered to buy them for him. Tim did not know the man.

"I suppose it's Ok if he knows mom."

3. But Tim had been told not to accept things from strangers.

Should Tim accept the candy from the man?

No. The man says he knows Tim's mom, but Tim is not sure. He doesn't know the man.

When he gets home, Tim should tell his mom what the man said. Tim's mom will then tell him if he is allowed to accept the candy from the man.

Only accept something from a stranger, or from someone you do not know very well, if your mom or dad has said that it is OK to do so.

Who's OK?

There are lots of kind people in the world, but some people are not so kind. It is not always easy to know who is kind and who is not so kind.

To be safe, never accept a ride from a stranger or from someone you don't know well. Don't be afraid to say "NO!"

NO!!!

Nicky, what are your safety tips?

"Never go off with a stranger. If you feel in danger, shout and run to a safe place. Talk to a parent or teacher about different ways to stay safe."

What Feels OK?

Last week, Jamie and Nicky's class talked about what feels OK and what doesn't feel OK. Nicky said surprises are really OK, even though she finds it hard to keep secrets — she nearly told Ben about his birthday present! Jamie said that you should always tell someone if something doesn't feel OK. Do hugs make you feel OK?

"Not more birthday hugs!"

14

A goodnight hug for sweet dreams.

◀ *Bad Touches*

There are some touches that make you feel cozy. But there are others that may make you feel uncomfortable. If that is the case, always tell your mom, dad, or another grown-up.

▶ *Hey, That Hurts!*

If you are playing and someone hurts you, tell the person to stop. If he or she doesn't stop, tell a grown-up.

Nobody should hurt you, by accident or on purpose. If it happens, tell someone.

▲ *Good Touches*

A good touch makes you feel happy and safe.

If you are told to keep a touch a secret, or if you don't like the touch, tell another grown-up.

A good touch should never, ever be a secret.

1. Ruby, John, and Kay were whispering.

2. Kay's babysitter was telling Kay to keep a secret about being hurt.

3. Kay was confused. The babysitter's secret made her feel uncomfortable.

Should Kay keep both secrets?

No. Good secrets about a surprise, like Ashya's party, should be kept.

But secrets that can upset or hurt you, or someone else, should not be kept. If a secret makes you uncomfortable, tell an adult you trust — perhaps your mom, dad, or a teacher.

Can you think of examples of secrets to keep and secrets to tell?

To Tell Or Not To Tell?

Even if you have been told how important it is to keep a secret, if it doesn't make you feel OK, tell a grown-up you trust.

Nobody should do or say things that may hurt someone else. For instance, saying nasty things about a person can be very upsetting. So if someone you know is feeling sad, why not be extra kind to them?

Jamie, can you keep a secret?

"No problem. But only if it's a nice secret. If a secret makes me or someone else unhappy, then I will tell a grown-up. And if, for some reason, he or she doesn't believe me, I will keep telling it, until someone does believe me."

Standing Tall

Marsha and Ben both know that bullying is wrong. Marsha was bullied and it made her very unhappy until she told a teacher who made sure the bullying stopped.

What do you do if you are being bullied, or if you know that someone else is being bullied?

Bullying is never, ever OK.

Bullying makes people very unhappy.

Girls should never bully anyone.

18

Boys should never bully anyone.

▲ Hitting Back

Some people think that hitting back at bullies is the way to deal with them.

But it doesn't work and it certainly doesn't make the problem go away. It can even get you into trouble.

The best way of dealing with the problem of bullies is to tell an adult you trust.

◀ ▲ Say No. Tell.

If you are being bullied, or know that it is happening to someone else, there are several things you can do.

You can say "NO!" to the bully. If that doesn't work, tell a grown-up who will know how to help you.

Don't be scared of telling. It is the bravest thing to do.

1. Tom was choosing people for his team.

2. Ann felt lonely and sad.

3. Raj didn't like the way Tom picked on Ann. He decided to stick up for Ann.

Tom is bullying Ann.

Bullying isn't just about hurting someone physically.

Making nasty comments about someone and leaving someone out on purpose is bullying. Making threats against someone or damaging his or her belongings is bullying.

Raj knows that all bullying is wrong. He wants to help Ann.

I can just ignore them.

No More Bullying!

Stop bullying by telling someone about it.

Some people can ignore nasty comments and stand tall. Bullies often get sick of being mean if nobody gets upset. But if that doesn't work, tell a grown-up.

In the end, telling will also help the bully. Bullies are often unhappy and need help.

I'm so glad I told you, Mr. Khan.

Ben, what can be done about bullying?

"Don't give up. Bullying is wrong so it is always right to tell.

Telling your mom, dad, or teacher will put a stop to bullying. It's also important to tell if you know that someone else is being bullied."

21

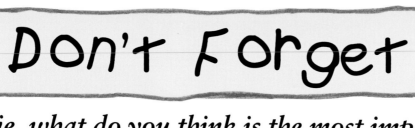

Don't Forget . . .

Jamie, what do you think is the most important thing about looking after yourself?

"The thing that matters most to me is telling the person who is looking after me how I feel. If I don't feel well, it's important someone knows. It's no good keeping it a secret, is it? It always makes me feel better if I talk to mom or dad about it."

Nicky, how do you keep safe and happy?

"I know that it is very important to say "NO!" if something doesn't feel right. It doesn't mean being rude. It just means being firm.

At school, we practiced saying "NO!" to each other. It was quite difficult, so I practiced at home in front of a mirror! And I know how to make an emergency telephone call."

Marsha, how do you stay healthy and happy?

"I keep fit and well by eating lots of healthy foods.

I really like playing soccer in the park. It's a lot of fun and it's healthy too! But after a game, I need to wash up!

When I'm playing, I know that it's important to think about what is safe. I always make sure that mom or dad, or the person who is looking after me, knows where I am.

Ben, what's your tip for feeling good?

"Some days I get grumpy if I've been yelled at. But being grumpy doesn't make me feel good, so I say sorry as soon as possible. Then I can stop feeling grumpy and can enjoy the rest of my day!

If I am angry with someone, I try to talk calmly to the person about how I feel. Then we can be friends again!"

23

Index

All the photographs in this book have been posed by models. The publishers would like to thank them all.

24